AGAINST ALL ODDS

To Kathy,

Best Wishes

Jeannette Johnson

AGAINST ALL ODDS

A Story
of the Miraculous
Gift of Life

Jeannette Johnson

Printed in the United States of America
Library of Congress Catalog Card Number:
2002112548
ISBN: 0-9676367-1-X (Paperback)
ISBN: 0-9676367-2-8 (Hardback)
Cover Design by Ed Tuttle
Edited by Dorian Kreindler

Heart Warming House
83 Ward St.
Manchester, NH 03104
www.heartwarminghouse.com

To my family, my friends
and everyone who shows
loving kindness toward
God's Creation

CONTENTS

ACKNOWLEDGMENTS 13

HIDDEN in the GARDEN SHED 15

ISABEL'S FAMILY 21

A CHANGE of HEART 27

CHASING BUTTERFLIES 39

DR. BELLMAN'S DISCOVERY 47

EMILY'S DELIGHT 57

A CHANCE to LIVE 63

A NEW FRIEND 71

BOOBOO'S ADVENTURE 77

SAYING GOODBYE 87

HOME at LAST 95

THE SCRATCHING POST INN 105

GLOSSARY 111

This tale is based on a true story
of an unusual cat.
Although some of the characters
in this story are fictional,
most of the events portrayed are real.

Jeannette Johnson

I am especially grateful to my
daughter Tracey for her love and
compassion toward animals
as revealed in this story.

Sincere thanks to Ed Tuttle for his
talent and hard work in creating
the cover design.

Special thanks to Dorian Kreindler,
Kathy Foote, and Kathy Fuller for their
encouragement, guidance,
and time spent on this book.

Most importantly, I'm forever
grateful to my God, who gave me
the ability to write this
heartwarming story about a
special kitten who wore
diapers.

CHAPTER ONE

HIDDEN in the GARDEN SHED

Ten-year-old Sarah Gibbons was frantically searching her bedroom for her favorite softball glove. An energetic young girl who enjoyed sports, Sarah had hoped to arrive at the field early enough to practice catching before the game began. Unfortunately, she couldn't find her glove. She looked through her bureau, under her bed, in her wardrobe, and behind her nightstand — but no glove. Baffled, Sarah thought, "Where can my glove be? I have to find it if I'm going to be catcher for my team today."

Racing down the stairs into the kitchen, Sarah collided with her mom, who was pouring water into their dog's water dish.

"Goodness, Sarah, what's your hurry?" asked Mrs. Gibbons, frowning while she brushed water off her jeans.

"Sorry, Mom," answered Sarah. "I'm looking for my catcher's glove and can't find it. Do you know where it is?"

Sarah's mom thought a moment, wiping specks of water from her eyeglasses. "Hum," she said, "it may be outside in the garden shed. Weren't you and Dad playing catch in the backyard Saturday?"

"Yes, we were. Thank you!" Sarah dashed out the back door, her ponytail bouncing from side to side. Beazly, her brown cocker spaniel, ran along beside her.

When she reached the garden shed, Sarah stopped short. She became suspicious upon seeing the door ajar and then grew fearful when she heard a strange, high-pitched, musical, chirping sound coming from within. Sarah's blue eyes grew very wide with fright, and she sought Beazly for protection. For a moment she didn't know what to do. Then slowly, with trembling hands, she pushed the rough, old door open and peeked inside, searching for the source of the sound. Beazly whined beside her impatiently and nudged Sarah's leg with his cold, wet nose as if he were prodding her to enter the shed. Reaching toward him, Sarah held her breath, took hold of his red collar, and courageously stepped inside with Beazly in tow.

It was dark within the garden shed and spooky. The eerie sounds continued, making Sarah shudder. While she paused to catch her breath, Beazly sniffed around the area in front of her.

Once her eyes adapted to the darkness, she listened nervously while searching her surroundings. Back in the far corner of the shed, beyond the garden tools, snow shovels, and lawn furniture, was Sarah's gray and white cat Isabel, whose green eyes peered back at Sarah and Beazly nervously. Six tiny, softly meowing newborn kittens snuggled between her and Sarah's softball glove.

"Oh, my!" exclaimed Sarah, partially covering her freckled face with her hands. "Isabel, you had your kittens! Look, Beazly,

Isabel had her kittens, and there're so many of them! Come on, Beazly, we have to tell Mom."

Upon hearing the news, Sarah's mother grabbed some cat food and an old brown army blanket from the trunk of her car. Sarah brought water, spilling most of it as she hurried. Beazly barked excitedly, as though he were announcing the news of Isabel's kittens to the whole world, while running along ahead of them.

As they entered the shed, Sarah and her mom had to remove two lawn chairs, a bicycle tire, a pair of old ice skates, and a garden hose before they could reach Isabel and her kittens.

"Well, Isabel, this is why I didn't see you today," said Mom, tenderly scratching Isabel's head. "You certainly have a fine family here."

"And they're so small," added Sarah. "And why are their eyes closed, Mom?"

"All kittens are born with their eyes closed, Sarah. Within seven to ten days their eyes will open, and then they'll be able to see."

Gently Sarah's mother lifted Isabel slightly to cradle her while Sarah placed the woolen blanket beneath her. Then she and

Sarah carefully arranged the six newborn kittens next to her.

"They're beautiful, Mom," remarked Sarah as she beamed with delight.

"Yes, they are," Mom answered giving Sarah a hug. "I'm sure they'll be more comfortable on the army blanket than crawling over your catcher's mitt. But, what I would like to know is how your glove got way back here?"

"I don't know, Mom. Do you think Isabel could've pulled it over?" questioned Sarah.

"It's possible, I suppose, but that will probably remain a mystery," said Mom, and rested her hands on Sarah's shoulders. "Anyway, let's leave Isabel and her kittens alone now, Sarah. I know she'll take good care of them."

Picking up her glove, Sarah peered at Isabel's new family. "Having kittens to play with is a lot more exciting than my softball game," she thought. "We're going to have fun together."

Slowly Mom closed the door, leaving it ajar the way Sarah had found it. They listened to the kittens' meowing melody for a moment before turning to leave. Sarah, thrilled with the new addition to their family, chatted busily to her mother as the two of them walked back toward their house with Beazly trailing along behind them.

CHAPTER TWO

ISABEL'S FAMILY

The following evening Mr. Gibbons brought home a big cardboard box for Isabel and her new feline family. After dinner Sarah helped her dad cut out a large opening in the box so Isabel and her kittens could enter and exit the box easily. Next, she and her mom placed cozy old towels in the bottom of the box for their comfort. Now they were ready to move Isabel and her newborn kittens into the family room, where they would be more comfortable. This idea thrilled

Sarah because she wanted to hold the kittens in her arms and play with them.

As soon as the mother cat and her family were settled in the family room, Isabel seemed happy. She kept close to her kittens, nurturing and caring for them, and the kittens stayed close to her. Isabel was a good mother. Sarah enjoyed listening to Isabel purr while washing each one of her tiny kittens as if she were singing them a song or telling them a story.

Within a few days the kittens' eyes opened, and they began to totter around their area, playing and jumping and sometimes growling softly. When it was nap time, they would sleep cuddled together, holding on to one another while they slept. They were a happy family.

Sarah was delighted to watch them maturing into playful kittens. She would sit on the floor with Beazly beside her and teasingly dangle a piece of paper on a string in front of them. The kittens took turns trying to catch the paper with their paws. Sarah chuckled, watching them balance themselves unsteadily on their hind legs as they attempted to reach for it. However, one kitten couldn't stand and swat at the paper like the others, but was just as playful chasing after it. Sometimes the kittens would lose their balance and fall backward on top of their siblings.

"Look, Beazly, did you see that?" she asked. Beazly looked up at Sarah, then rested his head on her lap and gazed at her intently as if to say "Yes, Sarah, but don't forget about me."

"Oh, Beazly, I think you're jealous," she consoled. "You don't have to worry, 'cause you know I'm still going to play with you too. . . ." Sarah paused, with a faraway look upon her face. "You know, Beazly, I think we should name these kittens."

She picked up the first gray kitten carefully and held him so Beazly could see him. "Look, Beazly, isn't he cute? What name should we give him? Since he's completely gray, do you think we should call him Smoky?" Beazly started to whine softly, responding to Sarah with his soulful brown eyes.

"Well, I guess that's a yes, so we'll call you Smoky," Sarah pronounced, patting his soft fur. His identical twin sister was attacking Sarah's wiggling toes when she picked her up.

"Now, what should your name be?" Sarah asked, holding the kitten up and examining her thoroughly. "I think we'll call you Mouse, because you look like a little gray mouse. Do you like her name, Beazly?" Beazly didn't respond because he was fast asleep. "I guess it's your nap time," Sarah admitted, yawning herself.

Still, Sarah continued naming the kittens. The gray and white kitten had longer fur than the others and a pretty face. She also walked with her head held high as if she were of a royal lineage, which gave Sarah the idea to name her Grace. "I think Grace is a perfect name for you," she proclaimed admiringly before kissing her and setting her down with the others.

The most playful kitten of the six was mostly black with four white paws. Sarah thought he looked like he was wearing boots, so she named him Boots. He was amusing to watch while he playfully jumped on Mouse and knocked her down. Then, growling, Boots bit her ear. Tickled, Sarah picked up Boots and scolded him softly, advising him not to be so rough as if he understood her.

The next kitten was mostly white with a little black on his chin that resembled a beard and he was more reserved. After pondering what his title should be for a while, Sarah chose the name Charles because she thought he looked important.

The last kitten to be named was mostly black with a little white on his belly and around his mouth. His white whiskers stood out in contrast to his black face. He was a handsome kitten — very lovable, and Sarah's favorite. She decided to name this kitten Slider because he was unable to stand up. He slid across the floor, pulling himself around on his front legs, with his hind legs dragging behind him. Fortunately he had been born with extra thumbs on his front paws, known as double paws, to help him get around.

Sarah's parents had also noticed that he had another problem: He couldn't tell when he had to use the litter box, therefore he would wet and mess everywhere. So her dad sectioned off a small area of the family room and placed a piece of old carpet on the floor. Even though Slider had problems, they didn't seem to bother him much. He was able to get around as well as his brothers and sisters and was just as mischievous.

CHAPTER THREE

A CHANGE of HEART

Early Saturday morning Sarah dashed about her house dressed in her blue shorts, yellow team shirt, and cap helping her mom take care of Beazly, Isabel, and the kittens. Sarah was excited that her team was undefeated, and waited with joyful anticipation for her dad to drive her to the park. But an unexpected telephone call delayed their leaving. This made Sarah impatient.

"Gee, I wish he would hurry up," she thought as she stood outside patting Beazly, trying to calm herself down. Attempting patience, she ran her fingers through his soft brown fur. She could still smell the lingering sweet scent of the shampoo she had used to bathe him the day before, which prompted her to bend down and put her arms around him. As she buried her nose in his fur, she imagined Beazly, Isabel, and the kittens at her ball game, scurrying through the grass and playfully chasing one another. What fun! This made her smile.

"Sarah," Mom interrupted her daydreaming. "Did you look in on the kittens?"

"No, I didn't, Mom, but I will," was Sarah's response.

Quickly Sarah ran to the family room and quietly walked up to the barrier. Peeking over, she found Isabel sleeping peacefully with her kittens. "Good," she thought, then turned and sped softly out of the room, through the kitchen door, snatching her baseball glove from the table, and reached the car at the same time as her dad. Together they hopped in and zoomed away.

"Perfect weather for a ball game," Dad remarked as he parked the car.

Sarah nodded, clutching her mitt with one hand and the door handle with the other. Quickly she jumped out and began to run toward the field.

"I know you'll do the best you can, Sarah, and that's important," Dad called to her. Sarah stopped, turned, and smiled, displaying the wad of pink bubble gum in her mouth as she shot him a thumbs-up. Then she continued as fast as she could toward the field to meet her friends and teammates.

As a first-time catcher this year, Sarah made an occasional mistake. Since she was determined to play her best, Sarah heeded all instructions and suggestions from her coach. Through her efforts and practice Sarah's performance improved giving her confidence. With this new confidence, her softball games became more exciting, challenging, and fun.

Once the game began Sarah relaxed and played well. She began to enjoy herself more and more with each passing inning. Time went by swiftly, and, before Sarah realized, the top of the fourth and final inning got underway. With her team leading by a score of three to one, Sarah started to focus a little of her attention to the sidelines and bleachers. She listened to her dad's voice coaching her teammates from the viewing stand and Beazly barking while she crouched behind home plate waiting for the next pitch. Glancing out of the corner of her eye, Sarah could see Beazly jumping up onto the fence as if he were trying to push it over, which would give him access to the field and the ball. Sarah smiled at the idea of him interrupting their ball game. For a moment her mind drifted to envision Isabel and the kittens on the field too — just as the ball landed in her glove.

"Strike three! You're out!" the umpire called as Sarah threw the ball back to the pitcher.

"One more out, and we'll win this game," she thought. "Then I'll be going home to play with the kittens."

Sarah sized up the next batter as the girl approached the plate. She was a tall girl, able to hit a home run easily if given the opportunity. With the bases loaded, Sarah and her teammates were feeling a lot of tension. Sarah kept her eye on the girl on third base, who was trying hard to steal home. The pitch came in.

"Strike one!" the umpire pronounced, while the batter repositioned herself. The second pitch came in hard into Sarah's glove. "Strike two!" the umpire hollered. Just as

Sarah was about to throw the ball back to the pitcher, it slid out of her glove and fell on the ground. Fumbling for the ball, she hurriedly picked it up and looked about. The girl on third base was almost home. Running as fast as she could toward her opponent, Sarah barely tagged her with the ball before the girl slid into home plate.

"She's out!" the umpire proclaimed.

Everyone on Sarah's team was cheering. This was game three of the season, and they were still undefeated. Sarah and all her teammates were happy.

Coach Harding was especially happy and grinning from ear to ear. A tall, slender man who wore his baseball hat so far down on his face that it almost covered his eyes. He was dedicated to his team and spent long hours coaching them. Mr. Cole, his assistant, was a short, husky man who donned his cap high on his head, ready to receive Coach Harding's directions. They cared deeply for their team players and made sure everyone had the opportunity to play during the games. Both taught their team valuable lessons on the game of softball, sportsmanship, respect, and team spirit. Their hard work exhibited itself in the team's performance and record of wins. This game victory thrilled them. So in appreciation, they bought all their players a drink at the concession stand.

Sarah's parents, also delighted, hustled over to the concession stand along with Beazly to meet and congratulate Sarah and her teammates. When Sarah saw all of them walking toward her, she started to laugh in spite of herself, seeing Mom wearing her straw gardening hat to keep the sun off her face, a white shirt, and denim overalls while Dad sported his team shirt from last year, which now barely covered his rounder belly. Dad smiled broadly as they approached Sarah, eagerly waiting to give her a hug and congratulate her. Beazly was so excited, he kept jumping up on her until she finally patted him. "Yes, Beazly, I'm glad you're here, I wish Isabel and the kittens were here with you too, but I know that isn't a good idea."

"Dad," Sarah said, "can we stop at the bicycle shop on the way home and buy a new basket for my bike?"

"What's wrong with the one you have?" he asked.

"It was badly damaged last week when I crashed, cause I turned too quickly to avoid a collision with Mrs. Smith's dog," she answered. "I still have a scab on my knee from scraping it against the curb."

"Well, I guess in that case we can stop — especially after the way you've been catching for your team," he replied. "We have to pick up your cousin Matt on the way home too. He'll be spending the afternoon with us."

Sarah groaned.

"Aunt Lillian and Uncle Mark are going to a wedding this afternoon, and they'll be picking him up at dinnertime," Mom advised, "so this will give both of you the afternoon to enjoy yourselves."

"The last time he came over I got in trouble because he decided to spray Mr. Perry's cat, Simba, with the garden hose and nearly drowned him before Mr. Perry yelled at him to stop," Sarah complained.

"We can suggest Matt bring his bike along with him to our house. It should fit in the trunk of our car. Then perhaps the two of you can ride your bikes to the park, which should make the afternoon more pleasant for both of you," Dad said.

Matt was one year older than Sarah. Tall for eleven, he had long skinny legs and bony knees and played Little League baseball. He was always bragging about his team and how well he performed as a player, probably because his long legs enabled him to run faster than many others. Sarah was not looking forward to spending the afternoon with him. Hopefully, Matt wouldn't be a brat this time.

After lunch her dad put Sarah's new basket on her bike while she and Matt got their gloves, planning to play catch together at the park. Sarah's mom had made chocolate chip cookies, Sarah's favorite, and had bagged some for them to take to the park. As her mother handed the cookies to Sarah, she asked, "Did you show Matt Isabel's kittens? I think he would love to see them."

"No, I didn't," she answered. "I didn't think he'd be interested."

"Isabel has kittens! Yah, I want to see them!" Matt sputtered, "I haven't seen kittens in a long time."

"Come on, I'll show them to you; they're in the family room," Sarah offered hesitantly, placing the cookies and gloves on the table before Matt hurried off in search of the kittens.

Isabel seemed nervous with Matt next to her kittens, so Sarah cooed softly to her, patting her fur to comfort and calm her.

Matt picked up Grace and held her in

his arms while she meowed. "This one is cute," he commented, holding her for several minutes. As he put her down on the floor, he noticed Boots, who had his front paws on Charles's back and was attempting to chew on his ear. "I think I like this kitten with white paws, though," he stated, picking up Boots. Immediately, Boots began biting his fingers. "Yah, I like this one. He's more fun. I'll ask my parents if I can have him . . . Gee, Isabel sure has a lot of kittens."

Matt suddenly noticed Slider and quickly put Boots down. "What's wrong with this one?" he asked, picking up Slider and examining him, tugging at his back legs. "He sure is funny-looking, and he can't stand up. Who would ever want to have a kitten like that?"

Slider's eyes were wide with fright as he struggled to escape Matt's grip.

"Please give Slider to me," Sarah pleaded.

"Why do you want him? He isn't good for anything," Matt provoked.

Sarah reached toward Matt, trying to get Slider away from him. "Give Slider to me!" she demanded.

"Yah, I'll give him to you after I watch

him drag himself around on the floor," Matt replied, and finally set him down.

"Hey, look at that goofy kitten go," he commented, laughing. Terrified, Slider dragged himself from Matt as fast as he could, trying to get far away from him.

Sarah, upset, ran over and picked up Slider and held him close to her, protecting him from her cousin. Tearfully she scolded, "I don't think you should pick on him just because he's different from the other kittens. How would you feel if people picked on you and laughed at you because you were different? In Sunday school we learned that the book of Proverbs says that what people like best about someone is their kindness. I really didn't want to show you Isabel's kittens because I knew you'd be mean to them."

Matt stared at Sarah for a long moment, then answered thoughtfully, "You're right, Sarah, I'm sorry; I was acting like a jerk. I never saw a kitten like that before, and he surprised me. Please forgive me."

Sarah felt something warm on her shirt and looked down to find that Slider had wet on her. Then she began to chuckle. When Matt realized the source of her amusement, he chimed in, and they both laughed together.

"Come on, Sarah, let's go to the park and play catch," Matt prodded.

"After I change my shirt," she answered, setting Slider down next to Isabel.

Matt and Sarah enjoyed the rest of the afternoon playing catch at the park, eating chocolate chip cookies, riding their bikes down to the ice cream stand and around the neighborhood. It was a perfect afternoon. Matt didn't brag once about how great a ballplayer he was or tease Sarah about Slider. He was nice to her, and they had fun.

When Aunt Lillian and Uncle Mark arrived to take Matt home, Sarah was sad to see him leave because they had become friends.

"I'll see you again soon," Matt assured Sarah, calling out the car window.

"Hope so," she replied as she stood waving goodbye with Beazley and her parents beside her. Sarah gave her dad a hug, her arms too short to fit fully around his belly. "You were right, Dad, it was a nice afternoon for both of us."

CHAPTER FOUR

CHASING BUTTERFLIES

Kittens mature quickly, and before Sarah realized it, eight weeks had passed since their birth. Sarah's mom had given them small rubber balls and catnip-filled toys resembling mice to play with. They delighted in their toys, especially the mice, smacking them about and tossing them into the air. It wasn't long before Boots had torn a hole in one of the mice spilling catnip on the floor. Dad was the first to notice Slider rolling in the pleasurable stuff only a cat could enjoy. When Sarah tried to pick him up, Slider swiftly dragged himself away.

"Humph," Sarah said disappointed, then turned to observe what the other kittens were doing.

Charles and Smoky snuggled together in a large cardboard box in the far corner of the family room, sleeping. Occupying the box with them was Mouse, their watch-cat, who busied herself sharpening her teeth and claws on the box edge. Suddenly Mouse stopped and looked across the room. What she spotted was Boots and Grace heading their way, crouching as they prepared to take over what she and her brothers enjoyed. Mouse stood bravely defending her territory from the two advancing kittens who came to claim the box as theirs. With their backs hunched and claws exposed, it turned into a scuffle. The combination of claws flashing, teeth biting, kittens meowing, and growling brought an end to the nap Charles and Smoky were enjoying, and they found themselves now involved in a rumble. Boots and Grace soon realized their charge was useless and quickly retreated, with Charles and Smoky in hot pursuit.

Victorious, Mouse held her head high and licked her paws before returning to her cardboard box, where she proudly continued sharpening her teeth and claws just in case there was another challenge.

All the toys, cardboard boxes, and a scratching post Mom had placed within their section of the family room to discourage the kittens from clawing the furniture helped. Nevertheless, despite her best efforts to remove everything the kittens could knock down or get hurt with, and building a barrier to keep them where they belonged, the kittens still managed to escape outside their assigned borders.

Early one morning Mom found Smoky and Grace meowing loudly while clinging to her lace curtains in the family room, trying to loose themselves from their predicament. Mom, who is afraid of heights, was bravely climbing up the stepladder to rescue them, when Sarah and Beazly entered the room. Suddenly, a chain of events happened, the likes of which they had never seen before or ever would again.

Boots, being the playful kitten that he was, began chasing Slider around the room. Mouse and Charles watched this action, and seeming to find it fun, joined in, chasing after Slider and Boots. When Beazly saw what was happening, he couldn't restrain himself and began barking, scaring the kittens, then following them. Terrified, Mouse, Charles, Slider, and Boots ran behind the sofa, clawing their way up the back of it and along the top in an effort to get away from Beazly.

Isabel, rudely awakened from her nap by all the noise and commotion realized her kittens were in trouble. Immediately, she sprang to her feet in a running position with her ears pressed back against her head indicating the seriousness of her attack. Her mouth opened wide revealing her teeth and fangs as she swiftly narrowed the gap with the unsuspecting canine. Rounding the corner of the sofa, Isabel intercepted the horrified barking Beazly with her right paw and exposed claws swiping the playful pooch across his nose.

Injured, Beazly yelped. Crouching with his tail between his legs and hurrying as fast as he could to leave this scene, backed into the stepladder that Sarah's mom was perched on while fleeing.

Mom, who was teetering on the stepladder trying to get Smoky and Grace down from the curtains, came close to being knocked off the ladder in this free-for-all. Frightened, Mom began screaming as she grabbed hold of Smoky and Grace. Valiantly she clutched the rescued, frightened kittens in her hands and was beginning her descent from the top of the stepladder when Charles and Boots went leaping past her, landing on top of the television set.

Swiftly Sarah ran to intercept the kittens before anything else happened and gathered them in her arms as quickly as possible before returning them to their area behind the barricade.

Mom was fuming — upset with the kittens' behavior, all the noise they made, and the mischief they got into. "I can't wait until next week when they'll go to their new homes! Then I'll have some peace and quiet around here!" she hollered before storming out of the room.

Sarah walked over to Beazly, who was hiding behind a large stuffed chair rubbing his nose with his paw. She knelt beside him and examined his wound, wiping the remaining drops of blood with the bottom of her T-shirt. "There, Beazly, I think you'll be fine now," she consoled.

Sarah plopped down on the floor next to him and wrapped her arms around his neck. She thought about all the things Mom had said before leaving the room. She was unhappy with the idea of losing her furry friends and would miss them. The kittens were a joy to her. When she came home from school, she immediately went to the family room. Upon seeing Sarah, they would run to her and play with her shoelaces or tug on her pant leg as if to beg "Pick us up." Now her thoughts were on the kittens' leaving and living elsewhere. This made her sad to think, they had only one week left to be together.

Sarah worried about Slider because Mom hadn't found a home for him. Mom insisted that he couldn't stay with them because he had too many problems. They tried to keep him and the other kittens in their section of the family room, but lately they would escape quite often. Once she'd found Slider sleeping on the sofa, which would have upset her mom had she known about it. Luckily he hadn't wet on it, or he might have been in trouble.

On Saturday Sarah gathered all the kittens into a carrier and brought them and Beazly outside into the fenced-in backyard. She played ball with them by rolling two small rubber balls on the ground. Sarah giggled while she watched all of them, including Slider, scurry after the balls. Occasionally she tossed sticks for Beazly to fetch, but he preferred to intercept the rubber balls meant for the kittens. At times Beazly got carried away while dashing about and nudged the kittens with his nose, flipping them over onto their backs.

Grace and Mouse also discovered amazing things outdoors. Their favorite seemed to be the bright orange and black Monarch butterflies flitting about her mom's flowers. Standing on their hind legs, the limber kittens resembled graceful, furry ballet dancers reaching toward the colorful butterflies with their front paws. These butterflies, however, eluded the kittens' reach and gave the appearance they were playing a game of Catch Me If You Can with the kittens.

Mouse, being adventurous and having lost interest in the butterflies, decided to explore a large patch of yellow daisies and sat down in the middle of them. Her nose level with the flowers allowed her to view a honeybee collecting pollen. Enchanted by the bee, she gently put her paw up and tried to catch it — not understanding the bee could sting her. Busy at work, the honeybee continued gathering pollen and flew away.

Meanwhile Slider was chasing after grasshoppers that were jumping through the grass. Soon Charles joined Slider in the grand chase, not noticing that Smoky and Boots were sneaking up on them, prepared to leap on their preoccupied brothers. Tuckered out, Slider rolled himself over on to his back to soak up the sun's rays and relax. He looked very comfortable in this position and was falling asleep when Boots came over and started a wrestling match between them.

When the kittens and Beazly lay down to rest on the soft grass, Sarah knew playtime was over. She collected all the kittens back into the carrier and returned them to the house. "Be good kittens and don't get into trouble," she advised, while depositing each one outside the carrier with a kiss. Sarah placed fresh water in their dish and gave them a few treats before leaving. Later, she peeked in to check on them and found five of them all curled up together taking their afternoon nap — with the exception of Slider. He was sleeping with his head resting on top of Boots. This was Slider's way of cuddling.

CHAPTER FIVE

DR. BELLMAN'S DISCOVERY

"Whoever thought catching a kitten would be so difficult," Sarah's mom murmured to herself, while chasing Boots around the family room with a towel in her hands. Finally she cornered the escape artist by throwing her dish towel over him, then scooped him up and deposited him into Beazly's carrier, along with his captured brothers and sisters.

"There, all I need now is the car keys,

and we'll be on our way for your appointment," she stated. Happily she entertained the thought that it was finally time for their checkup and the shots they all needed for adoption by their new owners. She didn't want to be late for this appointment. So Mom hurriedly grabbed her car keys, rushed out the door, put the carrier containing the kittens in the backseat of the car, and drove to Little Friends Animal Clinic.

Dr. Bellman owned this well-known establishment and had been the Gibbons family's veterinarian for a number of years. He was a friendly man, who wore a long white coat over his clothes. His graying hair was short, except for a few strands that he combed across the top of his head to hide his bald spot. Small reading glasses connected to a silver chain around his neck perched on the end of his nose.

"You can come in now, Mrs. Gibbons," called Gina, the receptionist, her smile revealing the dimples in her cheeks. Gina was dressed in a denim skirt and white T-shirt with a print displaying cats chasing mice, which reminded Sarah's mom of Isabel's active kittens.

Entering the examining room, Alaina, Dr. Bellman's assistant, introduced herself to Sarah's mom. She was a tall, slender and pleasant girl with dark features, and short black hair. Alaina recently began working with Dr. Bellman while she continued her studies to become a veterinarian. As she conversed with Sarah's mom in the examining room, she spoke highly of Dr. Bellman and his willingness to help her when she assisted him with the examinations. She confided that he took time to explain any problems he found with the patients they were examining and asked Alaina what she would recommend for treatments and why. This training was not only helpful, but a wonderful learning experience for which she was grateful to Dr. Bellman.

"Hello, Mrs. Gibbons," Dr. Bellman said, stepping into the examining room. "These must be Isabel's kittens," he said, lifting the carrier from the examining table and placing it on to the floor, then opening the carrier door to release the kittens. "It looks to me like she has a nice litter."

"Yes, she does," declared Mrs. Gibbons. "Except for one, who has a problem."

"Really?" Dr. Bellman answered, watching the kittens scamper out of the carrier and run about the examining room. Suddenly Slider pulled himself into view and quickly joined his siblings in exploring this new place.

"Oh, I see what you mean," Dr. Bellman remarked, studying Slider. "It's obvious this little fellow has something wrong with him. Would you mind, Mrs. Gibbons, if I took an X-ray of this little guy? I really would like to see what's going on here, and why he's like this."

"Please do," replied Mrs. Gibbons.

"Good, I'll be back in a couple of minutes," Dr. Bellman assured her.

During Dr. Bellman's absence the kittens romped around the examining room chasing one another and playing. This place was fun. Boots ran behind Alaina's feet and hid, as though he were playing peekaboo. Alaina laughed.

Mrs. Gibbons commented that she was glad the kittens were on the floor, because it would have been difficult trying to protect them from jumping or falling off the examining table while they waited for Dr. Bellman's return. Alaina knelt down on the floor next to the kittens. She couldn't resist the temptation to pick up Smoky and hold him in her arms. Grace also found this a great opportunity to climb up the back of Alaina's shirt and perch on her shoulder. Immediately Grace became interested in Alaina's jewel drop earrings, began batting at them with her paw, and attempted to bite them. When Dr. Bellman returned from x-raying Slider and witnessed this spectacle, he was in stitches.

Still smiling, he walked over to the X-ray viewer and placed the X-ray on it, studying it for a few minutes, before turning to address Sarah's mom.

"Mrs. Gibbons, I would like to explain to you what this X-ray shows is wrong with this little fellow. It appears that Slider's three lower vertebrae didn't connect correctly to his spine. This caused a hole in his spinal cord, which is why he's paralyzed, probably from the waist down." Continuing to study the X-ray, he added, "Unfortunately, there isn't anything I can do to correct this problem."

Dr. Bellman finished examining the kittens with Alaina's help and gave them their necessary shots, except for Slider.

Holding Slider in his hands, Dr. Bellman remarked, "This little fellow is a good-natured and cute kitten despite his disability."

"Yes, he is, but as of right now I don't have a home for him," Mrs. Gibbons shared. "I have homes for the others, but nobody wants a disabled kitten. Sarah wants to keep him, but I can't take care of a handicapped kitten. It would have to be a special person who would take him, and I'm not that person. Therefore, I have no other choice except to have him euthanized. If it weren't for Sarah, I would leave him with you now, but for Sarah's sake, I'll take Slider home with the other kittens. Then I'll bring him back."

Dr. Bellman shook his head slowly as he placed him down on the floor with the others. While he and Sarah's mom continued talking, Alaina stepped out of the room for a moment and returned with a technician named Tracey. Alaina wanted her to see Slider before Mrs. Gibbons took the kittens home.

"Isn't he the cutest kitten?" Tracey commented to Alaina, when she saw Slider for the first time playing with the other kittens. Watching him butt his siblings with his head and pull himself around as quickly as he could caused Tracey to smile with delight. Before leaving the examining room, she thought to herself, "This kitten is really special," and somehow she knew in her heart she would have to do all she could to intervene in Mrs. Gibbons decision.

"Then, I guess there's no other choice for this little guy," Tracey heard Dr. Bellman say as she left the room.

"Yes, I feel this is the right decision for him," Mom answered slowly.

Alaina helped Dr. Bellman put the kittens back into the carrier. She felt sad for Mrs. Gibbons and Slider. "I wish there were something I could do to help," she offered. "Tracey may know someone who would like to adopt Slider. She's helped find homes for some of the pets that people brought to us who were strays or injured and didn't have owners. Now that she saw how cute Slider is, I'm sure she'll try to find him a home.

"Thank you, Alaina," Mrs. Gibbons responded.

Before leaving the clinic, Mrs. Gibbons made an appointment with Gina to have Isabel spayed so she wouldn't have any more kittens. "This is Isabel's first and last litter of kittens," she told Gina. "They get into mischief and are too much work. Besides, I don't know what to do with Slider other than euthanasia."

"I'm sorry, Mrs. Gibbons, I'd like to take Slider home, but I can't because I already have three cats. I promised my mom I wouldn't bring any more home," Gina said.

"Thank you, Gina, for caring," Mrs. Gibbons replied.

Mrs. Gibbons drove home slowly from Little Friends Animal Clinic thinking about Sarah and Slider. She had made a difficult decision, and this troubled her, so she chose the longest route home. This allowed her time to ponder this situation.

By the time she returned with the kittens, Sarah had arrived home from school and waited expectantly at the door. "Hi, Mom," she greeted, opening the door to help with the carrier. Included in the welcoming party were Beazly and Isabel, although they were really looking for treats. Sarah took the carrier into the family room and released the kittens. She watched them play and chase one another.

"I'm glad you're home, and I'll bet you're hungry," Sarah uttered, filling their food dishes with kibbles, plopping down next to them on the floor, and petting them while they ate.

"I realize you'll be leaving soon to live with your new owners," she related sadly.

"It was fun having all of you here, and I'm sure going to miss you." Just then Slider crawled up onto her lap and stretched out. Rolling over onto his back, he looked up at Sarah with his sleepy eyes partially opened. Sarah rubbed his belly gently and scratched his head. Contented, Slider dozed off.

CHAPTER SIX

EMILY'S DELIGHT

By Saturday four of the kittens had already been placed in their new homes, and the Clark family was due to arrive any moment for Grace. Sarah had given her a bath earlier and was brushing her fur, thinking how pretty she looked, when the doorbell rang. She could hear her mom greeting the Clarks at the door and quickly brought the kitten into the kitchen to meet her new owners.

"This is my daughter, Sarah," Mom introduced.

"Hi, Sarah, this is Emily, and we're pleased to meet you," greeted Mrs. Clark.

Emily Clark was seven years old and very excited about the kitten. She had difficulty standing still because of her enthusiasm but listened carefully as Sarah explained the correct way to hold Grace. As she handed the kitten over to Emily, she held her gently in her arms listening to her purr. Emily's long dark hair covered Grace when she rubbed her check gently against the softness of her fur.

"Mommy and Daddy, Lily is purring," murmured Emily.

"Lily," repeated Mr. Clark, "that's a nice name for her . . . How would you like to take Lily home now, Emily?"

"Yes, Daddy," she answered.

"Then, we'll have to put her into the kitty carrier," declared Mr. Clark.

"I don't want to put Lily into the carrier, Daddy," she protested. "I want to hold her."

"Emily," Sarah stated firmly, "if you don't put Lily in the carrier, she could jump out of your arms while you're carrying her and run away. I'll put her into the carrier for you if you'll let me."

"Okay," Emily agreed, reluctantly giving Lily back to Sarah.

Safe in Sarah's arms, Lily purred. Tenderly Sarah lifted the kitten in front of her for one last look before she rubbed her face against Lily's head. Saying goodbye, she gave her a kiss, then gently settled her into the carrier, offering the kitten to Mr. Clark.

"Thank you, Sarah," said Mr. Clark, taking the carrier from her and holding it so Emily could see Lily inside.

"I hope you'll be happy with your new kitten," stated Mom while handing Mrs. Clark a small brown paper bag containing food and treats for Lily.

Emily, anxious to leave, placed her small hand next to her dad's on the carrier handle and asked, "Can we go home now, Daddy?"

"Yes, Emily, we can go home now," answered her dad. Opening the outside door in unison, they walked down the steps together toward the Clark's car.

Sarah strolled to the dining room window and watched the Clark family enter their car, fasten their seat belts, and drive off with Lily. With the kittens gone she felt sad. Slowly she walked back to the corner of the family room sectioned off especially for Slider, sat down on the floor, and held him. Beazly stretched out on the floor beside them, put his head onto Sarah's lap, and gazed up at her. His large brown eyes peered into hers as if to tell her, "I know you miss them, but I'm still here with you."

"Thank you, Beazly," uttered Sarah, with her voice full of emotion toward her companion.

Sarah closed her eyes, thinking back to the time Beazly and the kittens were chasing rubber balls in the yard and the fun she'd had watching them trying to catch butterflies and grasshoppers. She remembered all the mischief the kittens had gotten into, especially when they had found Mom's knitting bag and unraveled her yarn, as well as some of the sweater she had been knitting. They had tangled the yarn everywhere, including around themselves. Even though Sarah had tears in her eyes, she still smiled because of the good times she'd had with her furry friends.

With these wonderful memories still fresh in her mind, she picked up Slider and the rubber balls. Beazly jumped up, wagging his tail, because he knew what they were going to do. Sarah plopped her baseball cap on her head, and out they went into the backyard to play ball and have fun.

CHAPTER SEVEN

A CHANCE
to LIVE

Finally the day arrived that Sarah's mom dreaded most. She listened to Isabel, held captive within the carrier, complaining from the backseat of her car as she nervously drove to Little Friends Animal Clinic early that morning.

"Good morning, Mrs. Gibbons," Gina greeted, her broad smile beaming and her dark eyes twinkling. "What a beautiful day it is today."

"Good morning," she answered, even though she didn't share Gina's enthusiasm. "I'm leaving Isabel and her kitten with you today. We found good homes for all her kittens except Slider. I don't know what to do with him other than euthanize him. I can't keep him. Unless your clinic can find Slider a home, I don't think there's any other choice."

"Let me take them from you, Mrs. Gibbons, while you fill out the paperwork," counseled Alaina.

"Thank you," she replied.

Alaina decided to put Isabel and Slider into a cage farthest away from the barking dogs and closed the door. "You can stay together for now, until you have your operation, Isabel," she murmured. "Then we'll have to separate you from your kitten while you're recovering from surgery."

Isabel, upset by being locked in a cage, meowed loudly, while Slider, fearful of the noise and activity going on around him, huddled close to her.

Mrs. Gibbons, hearing Isabel's loud meows within the hallway of the clinic, tried to hide the tears in her eyes as she held the door open for a young lady who was carrying a box.

"Thank you," the blonde woman said as she hurried past her. Approaching the desk, she said, "I'm Nancy Whittier, and I came across this kitten lying on the side of the road not far from here as I was driving to work this morning. I think a car hit him. He's unconscious. One of the neighbors donated the towel he's wrapped in and suggested I bring him here. I couldn't leave him abandoned without helping him."

Gina took the box from Nancy and looked inside. Within the box lay a white kitten with a little brown on the end of his ears, whose head looked swollen. He seemed peaceful, neatly wrapped in a light green towel.

"Thank you for bringing this kitten to us. I'm sure the doctors will do what they can for him," Gina said, turning and handing the kitten to Alaina, who was standing next to her.

"You can call us later today, and we'll let you know how he's recovering and what the doctors found," offered Alaina.

Nancy thanked Gina and Alaina for their help and promised she would be calling them.

"You're a lucky kitten. I hope you'll be fine," Alaina sighed, carrying the unconscious kitten in the box down the corridor, to Dr. Rados's examining room. She thought how helpless the kitten looked as she placed the box on the examining table. After notifying Dr. Rados that there was an emergency, Alaina immediately reentered the examining room. The open white coat Dr. Rados wore over her khaki pants and pink cotton shirt revealed a stethoscope hanging from her neck, ready for use. Dr. Rados was a petite, energetic, gentle woman, who was very dedicated to her work. She lifted the kitten from the box and unwrapped the towel from around him. Dr. Rados worked quickly and quietly, examining the kitten for possible broken bones and other internal injuries, and monitoring his heartbeat. Occasionally she glanced at Alaina, who was assisting her. They worked well together as a team — Dr. Rados x-rayed the kitten, and Alaina developed the film.

After studying the X-ray, Dr. Rados returned to the examining room smiling. "Alaina, this little guy has a slight concussion and a cracked palate, but no broken bones or internal injuries — this information sure makes my day. He should be fine once he recovers," she shared with relief.

Alaina, also pleased with the good news, looked at Dr. Rados and smiled. She thought what a handsome cat he would become when full grown.

Dr. Rados then injected some antibiotics and other medicine into the kitten to help him fight infections and put some fluids back into his body.

"Now it's just a matter of time before he recovers, Alaina," she advised. "Please have Gina tell me when Nancy Whittier calls. I would like to thank her personally for bringing this kitten in."

Alaina gently picked up the unconscious kitten and carried him down the hall, placing him into the cage on the right side of Slider.

"What a busy morning," she thought. "I'll be glad when Tracey comes in to help us. She should arrive anytime now." No sooner had these thoughts entered Alaina's mind than she spotted Tracey Elder, dressed in green medical scrubs, opening the rear door to the clinic.

"Hi, Tracey," Alaina hollered to her.

Tracey smiled back in response. She was not only Alaina's working buddy, but her friend.

She and Alaina had discussed Slider's

condition earlier, and together they were trying to come up with a solution to help the little guy. At that time Tracey had told Alaina that she was looking for a home for him. Now, Alaina was anxious to find out the results of her efforts, which, it turned out, were not promising.

Tracey had been working at Little Friends Animal Clinic for a number of years and was a certified technician. A young, intelligent woman with long dark hair, ebony eyes, and a ready smile, she had a deep love for animals — especially cats — her favorite.

As Tracey walked by Slider's cage, she noticed him and stopped. Sadness gripped her soul as she looked at him through the bars of the cage. His small deformed body seemed out of place in such a large cage. Frightened, Slider edged himself against the back of the cage meowing, trying to hide himself. Slowly she spoke softly to him for a few minutes.

"Your mom is in surgery right now, and I have to help Dr. Bellman, so I can't take you out yet. But I'll come back later, and then we can get to know each other."

Slider looked back at her through his large copper-colored eyes and continued to meow shyly.

"I'll be back to see you later," she reassured encouragingly.

Tracey entered the operating room in time to prepare Isabel for surgery. She patted Isabel's gray fur while she lay anesthetized on the operating table. Tenderly she shaved her fur in a small area to prepare her for surgery. Dr. Bellman reentered the room just as she had finished.

"Isabel's ready for surgery, Dr. Bellman," she reported.

"Thank you, Tracey. It's been a busy day, and I'm glad you're here, because we really need your help," Dr. Bellman affirmed.

When Isabel's surgery was over, Tracey questioned Dr. Bellman about Slider. "Are you going to euthanize him?" she asked.

"Yes, we are. Mrs. Gibbons filled out the paperwork for that . . . unless you found a home for him, Tracey," he answered. "Besides, I agree with Mrs. Gibbons. The kitten has too many problems, and he'd be better off if we euthanized him. Don't you agree?"

"I'm sorry, but I disagree. Alaina, Gina, and I have talked about his condition, and we'd like to keep him for a while. He's a nice, friendly, healthy kitten, and we feel he deserves a chance to live. Maybe he could become a resident cat until we find a special home for him."

Dr. Bellman thought for a moment and replied, "All right, Tracey, if this is how you all feel, we'll put off euthanizing him for now. I'll have to discuss it with Dr. Rados, but I don't think she'll say no. I hope this decision will make you girls happy."

Tracey responded with a beautiful smile as she answered, "Yes, thank you."

She picked up Isabel and carried her down the hall to the cage to the left of Slider. Gently Tracey settled her inside and closed the door. It would be a while before Isabel would awaken from her surgery.

Slider, still frightened, waited for Tracey to leave and pulled himself over to the side of his cage closest to Isabel. Looking at her, he sniffed at her long fur sticking out through the bars of his cage, then rubbed his head against them, and meowed with relief. Putting his front paw through the bars, he touched her, as if he were trying to awaken her. After getting as close to Isabel as possible, he fell fast asleep.

CHAPTER EIGHT

A NEW FRIEND

"Well, it looks like you'll be having a friend," Tracey told Slider as she checked on the unconscious kitten in the cage to the right of him. "He should be waking up soon," she reported.

Even though Tracey was busy the rest of her shift, she walked by the kittens whenever she could and talked to Slider. Impressed by this kitten, she anxiously waited for things to slow down enough at the clinic so she could take him out of his cage and hold him in her arms. She felt sorry for him and wanted to comfort him and hoped he would feel secure if she held him. Finally the opportunity Tracey had been waiting for came.

Dr. Rados, Dr. Bellman, Alaina, and Gina had all gone home for the evening, leaving her in charge. She had taken the two dogs that were boarding out for exercise, cleaned their pens, and fed them. With all the animals, including a turtle named Useless, cared for, Tracey now had a moment to spend with Slider. While opening his cage, she engaged him in a soothing voice. She realized he had calmed down greatly since the morning and wasn't trying to hide from her.

"Hi, little guy," she reassured him lovingly. "Let me see you."

She noticed his large copper-colored eyes as he gazed at her from the far corner of his cage. His white whiskers curled downward and stood out against the black markings on his face. Tracey was still conversing with him while patting his soft fur when he rolled over onto his back so she could rub his belly. He thoroughly enjoyed the attention Tracey was giving him and continued to roll himself from side to side making sure she scratched under his chin, the sides of his face, and the back of his neck.

"Oh, look at you — performing like you were trained to do that," she commented, laughing. "You sure are a friendly kitten and a bit spoiled. Do you know what I think, little guy? I think you need a new name."

She pondered for a moment what special name he should have while she scratched his head and rubbed his belly, then arrived at a decision. "I know what your name will be," Tracey declared. "Your name will be BooBoo, because of your condition."

"How do you like your new name?" she asked, putting her head close to his. BooBoo butted her affectionately with his head. Picking him up, she continued, "Good, I think you like your new name. What a nice kitten you are, BooBoo. I know we're going to have fun together."

Holding him in her arms, she listened to him purr before putting him down on the floor. Immediately he began pulling himself around, investigating everything interesting to him.

Tracey allowed him to explore a certain area of the clinic while she finished the rest of her work. He seemed to be enjoying himself, crawling among the dirty laundry on the floor near the laundry bag. Suddenly he realized Nautilus the parrot was above him making a ruckus in his cage. He was the resident parrot and extremely spoiled. The technicians gave Nautilus crackers, apples, and grapes for treats, and now he was squawking for popcorn. BooBoo pulled himself under the bird's cage and looked up at him. He couldn't understand why this bird was squawking at him and calling him names. Tired of listening to Nautilus, BooBoo moved on to explore other things. Every once in a while Tracey would call him.

"BooBoo, BooBoo, where are you?" she summoned, and he would come to her and roll onto his back so she could rub his belly and scratch his neck.

"After I finish all my chores I'll have time to pick you up," she informed him.

Working quickly, Tracey cleaned up the mess from the day's work at the clinic, and then set up for the following busy day. She was relieved when she finally completed her chores and was free to spend time with BooBoo.

Tracey took an available small towel and wrapped it around his bottom.

"Now I can hold you without getting

wet," she confided. Picking him up, she held him close to her, feeling the softness of his fur against her face.

"What a nice kitten you are," she stated, patting his head. BooBoo began purring, happy in Tracey's arms, and once in a while butting her with his head. Perhaps this was his way of snuggling close to her. She held and talked to him for a while. When it was time for her to leave, she slowly reopened the door to his cage.

"I'm sorry, BooBoo, but I have to put you back into your cage so I can go home and take care of my own cats. They're waiting for me because it's their suppertime. I'll be back again tomorrow to see you. Here, I'll leave this towel with you so you'll be more comfortable," she shared.

BooBoo looked at her and meowed.

"Your neighbor should be recovering soon, and then you'll have a playmate. Hopefully it won't take too long to find both of you a new home. Until then you'll be staying here at the clinic with us."

Just before she left, she made out a card and attached it to his door. It read: <u>This Is BooBoo, Our Resident Kitten.</u>

Tracey stepped back from his cage and admired him. Yet the difficulty of locating a devoted person who would love him and have the patience to properly take care of him, troubled her. Pondering this she turned to leave.

"Good night, BooBoo — I'll see you tomorrow," she said, then turned off the light.

CHAPTER NINE

BOOBOO'S ADVENTURE

"Gina, did you see the card Tracey left on Slider's door?" Alaina asked. "She changed his name and replaced it with a new, interesting one," she remarked, opening up the door of BooBoo's cage to pet him.

"Are you hungry this morning?" she questioned, rubbing his chin.

Gina walked over to BooBoo's cage and read the card. "That's a different name for a kitten — but you're not an average kitten," she commented.

When he had finished his breakfast,

Gina wrapped him in a towel and picked him up. BooBoo snuggled close to her.

"You are a special kitten," Gina affirmed.

Earlier the two women had been discussing how they planned to introduce BooBoo to their clients. Now they were anxiously awaiting Dr. Bellman's arrival to tell him about their plans. Dr. Bellman had several surgeries scheduled, so it would be a busy day for them all. Alaina, dressed in her dark green operating scrubs, was ready to assist Dr. Bellman the moment he entered the office.

With a cup of coffee in his right hand and his briefcase in his left, Dr. Bellman bade the women a good morning as he arrived at the clinic. When Alaina told him what Tracey had named the kitten, he began to chuckle.

"What did you all name the other kitten?" he inquired.

"Alaina and I thought we should call him Oscar," replied Gina.

"Hmm . . . Oscar . . . that's quite a name for a kitten," he declared.

"Yes, we like it," Gina confirmed.

Immediately she became busy answering the telephone and making appointments. Later that morning she had time to introduce BooBoo to everyone who came into the office.

When Mrs. Gibbons arrived to pick up Isabel, she saw Gina carrying BooBoo around in a towel.

"Good morning, Mrs. Gibbons," Gina greeted her. "We thought you would be happy to know that we're going to keep BooBoo . . . Either as a resident kitten or until we find him a home," she announced enthusiastically. "He is greeting our clients this morning."

"Sarah will be delighted to hear this news," Mrs. Gibbons proclaimed. "Thank you; I believe he'll be happy here."

"Please tell Sarah he now has a friend named Oscar to keep him company. They're about the same age," Gina related.

During the morning Oscar awoke and tried to stand but was wobbly and fell back down. Even though he fell, he didn't give up but kept trying until finally he stood. Alaina was happy to see him awake and doing well.

"Good morning, Oscar. We've been waiting for you to wake up. I guess you probably have a headache this morning, but I hope you'll eat some breakfast anyway. It will give you strength. When you're feeling better, we'll put you in the same cage with BooBoo, but for now you'll be neighbors," she said.

Days went by before Oscar recovered totally from his accident. By this time BooBoo had become his friend and playmate, and they chased each other around inside the cage they had come to share. They were happy and no longer lonely because they were together.

When Tracey was on duty in the evening, she would let the two of them wander about the clinic and have a good time. She didn't object to the additional work BooBoo created for her, mopping up the streaks of urine and occasional feces he left behind.

BooBoo enjoyed watching Tracey wash the floor with a stringy cloth mop. He would lie still, watching the mop swing back and forth until it was close enough to pounce on. As he held tightly with his front claws, Tracey laughingly gave him a ride on the mop, gently swinging him and the mop back and forth.

One night, Oscar was busy popping bubbles with his paw in the wash bucket while Nautilus the parrot was squawking and screeching loudly at him. Curious,

Oscar stopped playing in the bucket, walked over to where Nautilus was, and sat down under his cage. With his tail twitching back and forth, and ears pointed straight up like antennae, Oscar listened to the parrot's piercing sounds. His eyes were focused intently on this bird as he watched every move Nautilus made walking and climbing within his cage. Nautilus continued squawking at Oscar — probably hoping he would go away. Oscar continued watching Nautilus plotting to grab him — until Tracey interrupted the action.

"I'm sorry, guys, but playtime is over for tonight," Tracey announced, picking up BooBoo and Oscar. "I know how you feel, Oscar: If only someone would let him out of his cage, then you would stop him from squawking at you. Don't worry; I'll cover his cage with a towel for the night so Nautilus will go to sleep. Then he'll be quiet," she assured him, putting the kittens into their cage together.

When Tracey walked up to Nautilus's birdcage, he was still squawking at her for more popcorn. "I don't have any more popcorn for you, but here are a few grapes. This should make you happy," she declared, covering his birdcage.

Before she left, she passed by the kittens' cage on her way out and stopped. Turning around, she walked back toward the meowing kittens and placed her hands on their cage. The kittens, hungry for attention and hoping to escape their confinement once again, rubbed their heads against her hands and fingers. "I'll see both of you again tomorrow . . . good night," she said. Then she left.

The next morning Tracey stopped at a toy store and bought some small toy trucks. She hoped the cart she planned to build would help BooBoo get around more easily. Tracey had learned about a woman named Mrs. Ryan from one of the clients at the clinic. She had a handicapped cat that used a special cart resembling a wheelchair. Watching the woman's cat pulling himself along quickly and easily with his front legs, while his back end rested on the cart, gave Tracey hope that the cart she was about to build would also be successful. In any case, she was anxious to try it. She had been talking with Alaina and Gina about making BooBoo a cart, and now was the time to do it. After arriving at the clinic and greeting everyone, she took out the toy trucks and showed them to the others. Excited, Alaina volunteered to help.

"I hope this cart will work, because it sure will help BooBoo get around easier," remarked Alaina.

"Yes, it will, and then he won't have to drag himself along anymore," agreed Tracey. "I hope he won't be frightened of it."

"We'll find out," Gina added.

During the afternoon, when things quieted down at the clinic, the three women gathered together in an empty examining room. Using the table, they disassembled the trucks, leaving the wheels on the red chassis. Gina held BooBoo in her arms and tried to calm him while he glanced around nervously. Alaina strung some string through the holes in the chassis and waited for BooBoo. Tracey and Gina held him in place on top of the cart and tried to keep him calm while Alaina wrapped the string around him. BooBoo's eyes were large with fright. Strange, loud, shrill sounds came from his throat resembling cries for help. When everything was tightly in place, the young women set him on the floor and let him go.

Go, he did! Terrified, he thought something was chasing him and headed for the door. Once in the hall, he turned left toward Oscar, their cage, and safety, trying to escape from the noisy cart attached to him. As he zoomed down the hall with the three women in hot pursuit, the cart hit the side of a wall, scaring him even more. Fearful the women would catch him, he escaped into Dr. Rados's examining room. Dr. Rados was examining a gerbil, when all the racket BooBoo made entering her room caused her to released her grip on the startled gerbil, allowing it to escape within the loose sleeve of her white coat and lodge near her elbow. Dr. Rados screamed and looked ill as BooBoo and his cart continued clattering around the table before leaving her room. He was moving so fast she barely identified him as he escaped between Tracey's legs into the hallway once again. Almost caught by one of the women, he and his cart skidded around the corner of the waiting room.

Meanwhile Mrs. Pierre, dressed in a professional dark blue suit with her auburn hair pulled back into a French braid, was bringing her miniature poodle, Fife, to the clinic for a checkup. They entered the waiting room at the same time as BooBoo. When Fife saw BooBoo and his cart coming at her, she yelped and jumped into her owner's arms. Unfortunately when this happened, Fife accidentally caught her toenails in Mrs. Pierre's hairpiece, flinging it to the floor in front of them. A startled and embarrassed Mrs. Pierre almost fell over as BooBoo flew by them once again, heading back toward Tracey and the other two women.

"Gina, what was that thing?" exclaimed Mrs. Pierre. Taking a deep breath and trying to compose herself, she put Fife down and picked up her hairpiece. "My poor Fife is trembling and panting so hard. I brought her in for a checkup, and now I'm afraid Dr. Bellman will have to treat her for shock."

Gina apologized to Mrs. Pierre, explaining how they were trying to help BooBoo, and she calmed down. She offered to help Mrs. Pierre reattach her hairpiece, and she accepted.

BooBoo's tongue was hanging out of his mouth, and he was panting rapidly when Alaina caught him in the hallway outside the waiting room.

"We're sorry, BooBoo," she consoled him, removing his cart. "We didn't mean to scare you. We thought the cart would help you get around easier."

Alaina continued petting him while

Tracey went to get a towel so she could pick him up and hold him. Tracey returned with the towel, commenting disappointedly, "Well, I guess that idea didn't work, but at least we tried."

After Tracey had held him for a few minutes and spoken softly to him, BooBoo calmed down. Nervously he continued looking about, not knowing what the women would do to him next. He could hear Oscar meowing from the safety of their cage as Tracey carried him down the hall toward it.

"Oscar, I'm returning your friend to you unharmed," Tracey declared as she put BooBoo back into their cage. Oscar ran over to his friend, greeting him by touching his nose against his. BooBoo then turned, looked at Tracey, and meowed.

"Don't worry, BooBoo, we're not going to put the cart on you again," she assured him. "I wish you weren't afraid of it. However, as long as you're happy, that's what's important."

CHAPTER TEN

SAYING GOODBYE

As time passed, BooBoo became a celebrity at Little Friends Animal Clinic. He enjoyed all the attention he received from Gina, Alaina, and Tracey, who continued to carry him around wrapped in a towel. His personality also won him the affection of the two veterinarians who allowed him to drag himself about the treatment rooms as long as the girls cleaned up after him. Many of the clients he greeted at the clinic were won over by his natural charm. In short, BooBoo was a lovable kitten that delighted in having his new friends, young and old, pet him, scratch his neck, behind his ears, and his head until he rolled over onto his back so they could rub his belly. And, being treated this way repeatedly, BooBoo became spoiled as a result of all the love and attention given to him by his friends.

Occasionally, BooBoo would get sick and have a temperature. During this time he stayed in a cage separated from Oscar for a few days and was given medication. Oscar would meow for his friend and playmate, but BooBoo lay on the bottom of his cage and slept. He was just too sick to play.

Concerned clients and friends asked about him if they didn't see him when they arrived at the clinic. Gina, Alaina, and Tracey explained that BooBoo had a bladder infection from not emptying his bladder properly and had to stay in his cage until he got better. During these times he needed a lot of care. The technicians checked on him often, walking by his cage to monitor his progress. Even though he was sick, BooBoo purred for these women when they petted him. He never scratched or growled when they were taking a blood sample or giving him pills to swallow. It amazed Alaina and Tracey how good-natured this kitten was.

Tracey worried about BooBoo because of his health problems and the special care he needed. She felt the clinic was not the best place for him to live. He needed a better place. What he required was a cat-lover's quiet home with someone to care for him. Unfortunately, she was unable to find one that would meet his needs . . . until . . . one day she realized that her new home and business were the answer to her prayer.

She had recently opened an inn exclusively for cats on a quiet country road. This gave her friends and clients a place to bring their cats while they were away on vacation. She had also just completed an associate's degree from the University of New Hampshire specializing in small animal care. This meant that she was qualified to be responsible for a cat like BooBoo, or other cats needing special care. Within the past two days, Dr. Bellman had spoken to Tracey once again about euthanizing BooBoo because of his health problems. This upset her — she wanted BooBoo to live. At that moment Tracey promised herself she would surely take care of him for the rest of his life.

Tracey met with Dr. Bellman, Dr. Rados, Alaina, and Gina the following day and told them she wanted to take BooBoo home to live with her. It didn't take long for all of them to agree with her plans. They believed BooBoo would be happy and well cared for living with Tracey, and they were happy for both the kitten and her. This made Tracey excited and happy, and she hummed throughout the rest of the day while waiting for the end of her shift. This was the day she had waited for — when she and BooBoo would go home together.

Oscar was also leaving the clinic later that afternoon for his new home, having been adopted by an older woman named Mrs. George. This lady already had a kitten named Samson about the same age, who was lonely and needed a friend to play with, chase around, and keep him company. Mrs. George thought Oscar would be perfect for him and hoped they'd have fun together while she was away from home working.

"Things aren't going to be the same around here without the kittens," Gina told Tracey.

"That may change at any time; you never know when someone will come into the clinic with another animal to rescue," Tracey responded.

"You're right. Life here at the clinic sure isn't boring," Alaina interjected.

One problem Tracey had to solve before taking BooBoo home was what she would use instead of a litter box. She had been mulling over her options and decided to buy some disposable diapers. That afternoon she went to a grocery store and looked at all the different types and sizes of diapers for sale. She chose the newborn size and hoped they would fit. Now she was anxious to get back to work and show them to the two other women.

Alaina and Gina thought diapers were a great idea.

"These should not be as difficult to put on BooBoo as the cart was," ventured Tracey.

Gina left to get BooBoo from his cage and found him enjoying his afternoon nap next to Oscar. "I'm sorry to awaken you, BooBoo, but we have a surprise awaiting you. I realize this is the last afternoon nap the two of you will be having together, but I'll be returning you to Oscar soon," Gina encouraged while picking BooBoo up.

Alaina and Tracey were discussing where to cut the hole in the diaper for

BooBoo's tail when Gina returned and gently laid him down on the examining table.

Tracey held up the diaper so he could see it. "Look what I bought for you, BooBoo," she uttered lovingly. BooBoo looked at Tracey and made a soft cooing sound in return while rubbing his head against her hand, not paying any attention to the diaper.

"I hope you won't mind these too much," she said. Tracey picked him up and held him while Alaina marked the hole for his tail. Once the diaper was ready, she laid him down on the examining table. Alaina rubbed his belly and talked to him, holding him still while Tracey put the diaper on. The idea that they were diapering a kitten instead of a baby seemed funny to all of them, and suddenly they all burst forth in peals of laughter. This made it more difficult. BooBoo's eyes grew wide because he didn't know what these women were doing to him, yet he lay still until they had finished.

Chuckling, Tracey picked him up and tested the diaper to be certain it would stay on. "BooBoo, don't you look cute in your diaper, and you smell sweet too," she announced. "Now you can go everywhere, and I don't have to worry about you wetting on me, the furniture, or anything."

Gina snapped a picture of him with her camera for their bulletin board so all his friends would be able to view him in his diaper. Then Alaina picked him up and paraded around the clinic showing everyone. Dr. Bellman and Dr. Rados considered the diaper a marvelous idea. "You gals should have thought of this sooner," they advised laughing. "He's still a celebrity here at this clinic."

Within one month's time BooBoo had truly become a well-known kitten at Little Friends Animal Clinic, and tonight he would be leaving to go home and live with Tracey. Alaina and Gina considered BooBoo special and had enjoyed him and Oscar immensely while the kittens lived at the clinic. At times it had been fun and sometimes challenging. Although they were both sad to see them leave, they were grateful for being involved in their lives.

Once the clinic's office hours were over, Tracey hurried to finish the work she had to complete before leaving. The prospect of bringing this unusual and special kitten home was thrilling to her.

"BooBoo, are you ready to go home?" Tracey asked.

BooBoo looked up at her with his large

copper eyes and made a cooing sound as if to say "Yes, I am."

"You won't have to come back here again unless you're a patient, and I hope that won't be very often because I'll take care of you," Tracey informed her courageous kitten. "We'll invite everyone at the clinic to come and visit you at our inn."

She picked him up and held him close for a few minutes before placing him into the carrier. Promptly closing the carrier door, she peeked in at him through the holes and smiled. Before turning off the light, she sighed, "BooBoo, let's go home."

CHAPTER ELEVEN

HOME at LAST

That evening Tracey drove slowly along the scenic country road leading toward the inn and BooBoo's new home. As she neared her residence, she noticed that darkness had graced the sky above them and wondered how the summer was passing so quickly. She enjoyed the warm evenings: arriving home while it was still daylight meant she could take an evening stroll or ride her bicycle along a trail nearby. With the passing of summer meant dark evenings, cooler weather, and then snow, which she didn't care for, because of the cold temperatures that accompanied it. Still, for now, she would enjoy the last days of summer with her special kitten she was bringing home.

"BooBoo, we're almost home," she said, as she rubbed her hand near the opening of his carrier. She was hoping to get a response from him, but BooBoo remained quiet. Floodlights lit up the yard as she entered her driveway and parked. The wind was gently blowing, causing the cat flag by her office door to sway in the cool August night. A sweet fragrance of freshly mowed grass, summer flowers, and sounds of crickets chirping all filled the air as she strolled along her garden walkway toward her office carrying BooBoo.

"BooBoo, I know you're going to be happy here at our inn," Tracey affirmed. "It's quiet, and you won't be scared by barking dogs like you were at the clinic."

Lifting him out of the carrier, she held him up so he could see his new home. He seemed frightened and upset, releasing loud, complaining meowing sounds from deep within his throat.

"I'm sorry, BooBoo, you're afraid but I know you'll be happy after you've been here awhile," she encouraged, trying to calm him. "This is my office. You can visit with me here and greet our guests. Do you think you would like to do that? I spend a lot of time in this office and in the two cat rooms I'm going to show you," she continued.

He seemed confused. His large copper eyes appeared to be taking everything in while she carried him around. She opened the screen door separating her office from the large cat room and entered, carrying him.

As they started to mosey over toward the three large condos on the far side of the room, the cats boarding inside the condo began to meow . . . but BooBoo meowed louder.

Tracey cuddled him close to her so he would feel safe in her arms.

"BooBoo," she coaxed gently, "these cats are our guests and will be staying with us for a few days. They're really nice cats, and you don't have to be afraid of them. Right now they're waiting for me to let them out of their condos so they can roam around the room. But first I want to show you what we have here that you can enjoy along with them."

She ambled over to a tall cat tree and placed BooBoo on one of the large carpeted resting spots attached to it and scratched his head and rubbed his belly. He seemed to enjoy his resting place on the colorful wooden tree covered with rope and soft carpeting. There were several resting platforms attached to this tree for cats to climb and jump, although BooBoo seemed contented stretched out on the platform he was on. Since the cats within the condos were still meowing, Tracey picked him up and carried him toward the screen door of her office. After passing a large picture window with a padded window seat in front of it, she stopped. "BooBoo, when you're familiar with your new home, you'll enjoy lying up here during the day and watching the animals outside and the birds feeding at the bird feeder."

As she opened the screen door to her office, she kissed BooBoo on his head before setting him down on the office floor. "Stay here and watch me while I take care of our guests," she instructed, as she reentered the large cat room.

BooBoo peered through the latched screen door, studying every movement Tracey made. He made short chirping sounds as she walked over to the three adjoining condos in the far corner. These condos had removable walls in the upper sections, so the five meowing cats inside — known as the De Sandra Gang, after their owner's surname — could wander about within their spacious, living area. This cat family had a warm response to the sound of Tracey's voice as she greeted them by rubbing against their condo doors.

"I'm sure all of you would like to come out for a while," she ventured, opening the doors. Skitters, a small, thin, black and white cat was first, followed by Amber, a beautiful, seal point Siamese. Tipper, the brown tabby cat, waited for Tracey to pat her first before jumping down onto the floor. Junior wasn't sure he wanted to leave his cozy bed in the loft. With a little coaxing from Tracey, this slinky, black cat came down to see her. He was an older cat and not as adventurous as the others. Responding to Tracey's voice and tenderness, he rubbed against her and soaked up all the attention she gave him. When Bandit — the boss cat from this group — a large white cat with black face markings, saw BooBoo, he ran over to the screen door to challenge him. Fortunately BooBoo was safely on the opposite side of the door and backed away from it when he saw Bandit approaching him. Skitters and Tipper didn't pay any attention to Bandit and BooBoo because they were busy playing with cat toys, pushing them around on the floor, throwing them up in the air, and catching them with their paws. Tracey began rolling small rubber balls for them to chase, and soon Bandit decided that looked like fun and joined in, leaving BooBoo alone. Amber and Junior perched themselves on the cat trees surveying all the activity by swinging their heads back and forth while focusing their attention on the others.

Before returning to her office, Tracey cleaned the De Sandra Gang's litter boxes, filled their food dishes with kibbles, and gave them some fresh water. She left the doors to their condos open to allow them to enjoy themselves in the large cat room for the night.

In the meantime BooBoo busied himself exploring Tracey's office; he crawled beneath her computer desk and under her sofa and chair, then made himself comfortable on the carpet while he waited for her.

Tracey entered her office quickly, trying to escape from the De Sandra Gang without letting any of them into her office behind her, and latched the screen door. Sometimes this was difficult, but tonight they were enjoying themselves with their toys and didn't run after her.

"Well, BooBoo, what do you think of your new home?" she asked, scooping him up. BooBoo meowed softly.

"Now I want to introduce you to Tigger, who's in the smaller cat room on the other side of my office. He lives here with me at the inn and is a nice cat like you. You should get along with him just fine."

Tigger was a handsome, silver-spotted tiger cat that had come to live with Tracey earlier that year. Like Oscar, someone had brought him into the clinic for care after being hit by a car. When he was better, Tracey had brought him home to live with her. An older and extremely gentle cat, he bonded very well with other cats who were guests at the inn.

Tigger, who was sleeping peacefully on one of the platforms of his cat tree, opened his eyes when she walked into the room. Stirring, he looked up at her when she approached him.

"Hello, Tigger," Tracey greeted. "I brought you new friend. This is BooBoo, who will be living with us. Right now he's frightened, but he'll calm down soon."

Tigger put his nose close to BooBoo to sniff him by way of introduction. BooBoo, unfortunately, wasn't as friendly and hissed back at him. So Tigger backed off, jumped down onto the floor, and began rubbing up against Tracey's legs to remind her it was his suppertime.

"Yes, Tigger, I know you're hungry," she acknowledged. "As soon as I change BooBoo's diaper, we'll all eat."

Tracey wasn't sure how difficult this task would be without the help of Alaina and Gina. But she found when she used Tigger's resting platform as a changing table, he cooperated with her, allowing her to change him without any difficulty at all.

"BooBoo, you're so good; now let's go inside our house and eat," she stated, bringing him and Tigger up the stairs and through the door separating her house from the inn.

Giving both of them a generous portion of food in separate dishes, Tracey placed Tigger's dish on one side of the kitchen and BooBoo's dish near her, while she enjoyed pizza and the company of her furry friends.

When dinner was over, she picked up BooBoo and moved him into the living room, with Tigger following close behind. It was time to relax and watch television. All three of them cuddled together on the sofa, with Tracey in the middle. Tigger was the first one to fall asleep curled up next to her while BooBoo sprawled out on his back in a soft blanket Tracey had wrapped him in. She rubbed his belly gently until he, too, fell fast asleep. He looked gloriously peaceful lying there with his front paws resting on his chest.

"Yes, BooBoo, you're going be happy here with Tigger and me. Regardless of your problems, I'll take care of you. I know some people had trouble looking past your disability and seeing what a wonderful kitten you really are. I'm sure happy you're here with us. You're a special kitten, and I love you." She lifted him slightly while he slept, bent down, and kissed him on top of his head. Softly she added, "BooBoo . . . you're home at last."

CHAPTER TWELVE

THE SCRATCHING POST INN

Three years have come and gone since BooBoo went to live with Tracey and Tigger at The Scratching Post Inn. He's officially part of the welcoming party, greeting guests in her office and winning their hearts with his charm and performance.

Maturing into a healthy, handsome cat, he has developed larger than normal upper-body muscles because of his condition, which allows him to climb anything he can get his claws into, including cat trees.

BooBoo and Tigger are the best of friends and chase each other around, along with some of the other guests, in a large outdoor yard. Tracey doesn't have to worry about cats wandering away or being chased by dogs in this safe, specially, enclosed yard. Lying in the sun enjoying themselves, chasing bugs, grasshoppers, or one another, Tracey's furry friends have the sense that they're permanently on vacation.

Often, Chippy the chipmunk entertains them on the opposite side of the fence by scurrying back and forth to gather birdseed. Perching on a stone outside of their reach, Chippy will eat the delicious birdseed while training his eyes on the cats, enjoying the chance to tease them. BooBoo, Tigger, and company line up along the fence and watch the show. With their tails twitching back and forth and making chattering noises, the cats follow every move Chippy makes, thinking how wonderful it would be to catch him.

One morning, Chippy or one of his friends got too close to the fence and a waiting cat. Tracey, sitting at the desk in her office, heard the chipmunk squealing for his life and ran to his rescue. Tracey pursued Tigger, causing him to release his grip enough to let the chipmunk escape. The disoriented chipmunk then headed in BooBoo's direction, where the frolicsome feline was waiting on the sidelines hoping to have his turn with him. BooBoo raced to grab Chippy, caught his claw in the chipmunk's tail, and hoisted him up off the ground. Drooling, BooBoo prepared to grasp him with his fangs — when Tracey arrived and spoiled the fun. Relieved, the chipmunk flew as fast as he could through the fence to safety in a nearby stone wall and home. Tigger, galloping in hot pursuit with BooBoo tagging feistily behind, looked so disappointed when they reached the fence and watched Chippy disappear within the stone wall. Tracey, however, pleased that the chipmunk had escaped, returned to her office smiling.

Whenever she has the opportunity, Tracey visits the cats outside in their yard and enjoys the warm morning sun relaxing in her beach chair with a cup of coffee, surrounded by her furry friends. As soon as she sits down, one of her friends will jump on her lap while the others gather around her craving attention. Since Tracey no longer works at Little Friends Animal Clinic, she's able to devote more time to the cats and her business at the inn.

When autumn arrives and the fire-colored leaves flutter down from the trees above their yard, the cats dash about trying to catch them before they reach the ground. As the dead leaves collect and are whisked about by the wind, Tracey enjoys watching her pets frolicking amid the whirlwind of leaves. How entertaining are these graceful cats, making the soul merry.

Winter brings even more adventures for the pets. Before BooBoo can go outdoors to play in the snow, Tracey dresses him in a pair of leather snow pants resembling a pair of chaps to protect his hind legs from the cold. The beauty of falling snow in the winter gives the cats a chance to explore the white, fluffy, crystal snowflakes. It doesn't take long for the cats to become covered with these glistening flakes after scampering about the yard. Then, cold and wet, they happily enter the inn, where they can find their favorite place to dry off, cuddle up, and go to sleep.

BooBoo is very contented living at the inn with his friends and Tracey. In the evening, when she and BooBoo relax and watch television, he climbs up on the sofa beside her and stretches out. Wrapped in his favorite blanket, he falls asleep.

Even though his health problems are under control, BooBoo still requires special daily care. Once a week Tracey bathes him in the sink. Afterward she towel-dries him, then blow-dries him on low heat, which BooBoo doesn't seem to mind. She has found that bathing him helps prevent bladder infections. Now that he is full-grown, this special cat has graduated to wearing medium-size diapers.

During the afternoons, BooBoo often lies on the window seat in front of the picture window being entertained by inquisitive birds, chipmunks, and squirrels chasing one another around outside or eating birdseed and peanuts at the bird feeder. Sometimes Tigger joins him on the window seat, where they cuddle together in the afternoon sun and nap.

Everyone who comes to The Scratching Post Inn and knows BooBoo loves his gentle nature and charm. He is truly a special cat — happy — and unconditionally loved.

GLOSSARY

Antibiotic: a medicine used to fight off bacterial infections.

Bladder: an internal organ in animals and humans that temporarily holds urine before the urine is emptied as waste fluid.

Catnip: a plant related to mint that cats are stimulated by.

Client: a customer of a business.

Condo: in this book, a comfortable multiunit structure for cats to live in while their owners are away.

Disabled: unable to perform or function normally.

Euthanasia: the act or practice of injecting a chemical into an animal or human, usually for the purpose of mercy killing, such as in cases of terminal illness or crippling injury; verb, euthanize

Spayed: to be made sterile, or unable to reproduce offspring, through a surgical operation; <u>spayed</u> for female animals. Synonym: castrated.

Palate: the roof of the mouth.

Ponder: to think about something thoroughly; weigh a matter.

Preoccupy: to completely absorb the attention.

Resident: a person or creature that lives at a particular place.

Scratching post: an often carpet-covered post where cats scratch or dig to sharpen their claws.

Spine: the backbone and central column of the skeleton, which gives strength and support to the body.

Spinal cord: the cord of nerves surrounded and protected by the spine that, together with the brain, comprises the central nervous system and is involved with sensory and motor impulses.

Stethoscope: a listening tool that helps a medical doctor hear the heartbeat, lungs, and other internal organ sounds.

Technician: a trained specialist.

Totter: to wobble or shake as if about to fall; stagger.

Unanimous: all in agreement.

Vertebra: one of many bony sections of the spine or backbone; plural, vertebrae.

X-ray: a photograph taken by a special camera that reveals internal organs and bone structure

About The Author

JEANNETTE JOHNSON is a loving and supportive wife, mother, and grandmother who lives in New Hampshire with her husband, Roger. Having a distinct fondness toward animals, she's blessed to know, love, and care for the special kitten mentioned in this book. Grateful for the kindness shown toward him, she knew others would enjoy knowing this remarkable story.

Against All Odds: A Story of the Miraculous Gift of Life is a heartwarming tale inspired by the true account of a handicapped kitten left at an animal clinic to be euthanized. This precious kitten's charm and gentle nature will utterly disarm and captivate you, as it did the three young women working at the clinic who rescued him. This story will leave you, the reader, breathlessly in love . . . and in awe. . . .